# THE CENTRAL SCHOOL OF SPEECH AND DRAMA

## UNIVERSITY OF LONDON

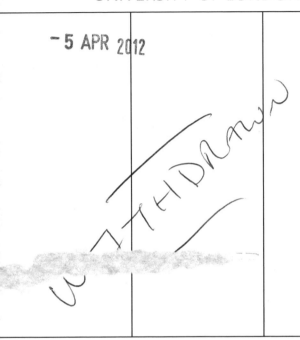

- 5 APR 2012

**Please return or renew this item by the last date shown.**

**The Library, Central School of Speech and Drama,
Embassy Theatre, Eton Avenue, London, NW3 3HY
http://heritage.cssd.ac.uk
library@cssd.ac.uk
Direct line: 0207 559 3942**

# CABBAGE
## original solo scenes

## HEATHER STEPHENS

*with a new adaptation of*
*Robert Browning's*
THE  PIED  PIPER

DRAMATIC LINES, TWICKENHAM, ENGLAND
text copyright © Heather Stephens

This book is intended to provide performance material for speech and drama festivals, examinations and workshops or for use in schools and colleges. No permission is required for amateur performance.

Application for performance by professional companies should be made to:

Dramatic Lines PO Box 201
Twickenham TW2 5RQ
England

No reproduction, copy or transmission of any part of this publication may be made without written permission of the publisher.

A CIP record for this book is available from the British Library

ISBN 0 9522224 5 0

Cabbage first published 1994 by Dramatic Lines, Twickenham, England. All rights reserved

Printed by The K&N Press Ltd., West Molesey, Surrey, England

to Louise and Nicholas

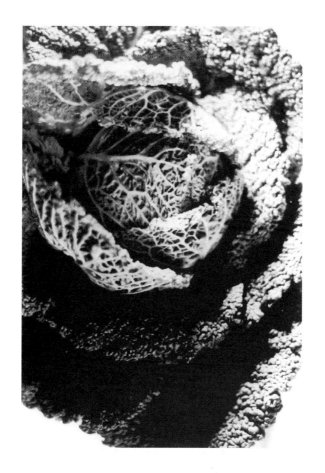

Acknowledgments
My very grateful thanks to:
Shaun McKenna, Principal of Examinations, LAMDA
Penny Phillips, EnsorSpeak
for their invaluable advice and encouragement
and to:
Jenny Thornton for the work involved
in the trial of scenes

# CONTENTS

# ABERFAN PROPHECY

**ERYL MAI DIED WHEN A SLAG HEAP SLID DOWN THE WELSH MOUNTAINSIDE ON TO PANTGLAS JUNIOR SCHOOL, ABERFAN ON OCTOBER 21ST 1966, SMOTHERING MORE THAN HALF THE 240 PUPILS. TWO WEEKS BEFORE THE TRAGEDY ERYL MAI HAD A PROPHETIC DREAM.**

*A TABLE LAID FOR BREAKFAST, CHECK TABLECLOTH, SOLID PLAIN CHINA AND A TEAPOT WITH KNITTED COSY. ERYL MAI SITS AT THE SINGLE PLACE SETTING STARING DOWN AT AN UNTOUCHED BOILED EGG SURROUNDED BY THICKLY-SLICED TOAST SOLDIERS AND A FULL GLASS OF MILK.*

**ERYL MAI:**  (Looking up)
Mammy!
(Pause)
I'm not afraid...
(Pause)
...Really not afraid to die!

*ERYL MAI BUSIES HERSELF WITH THE EGG*

I understand what I'm saying, Mammy.
Really, I do!

*ERYL MAI BUTTERS TOAST IN MATTER OF FACT FASHION*

Why talk of dying?
(Continuing to butter toast)
Why talk of dying and me so young?

*ERYL MAI LAYS THE KNIFE ASIDE*

Because of the dream last night:
the vivid dream.
(Quietly insistent)
No! Mammy; listen!
You must **listen!**
(Pause)
Please!
(Pause)
To speak of death at breakfast might be
...'Bad-manners'
but this needs to be said, you understand.
(Pause)
I walked to school, same as always...
...but there was no school there.
In my dream, that is!
(Pause)
Hear me out, Mammy!

*ERYL MAI QUIETLY STANDS AND MOVES UP CLOSER TO MOTHER*

Of course you are busy;
I see that for myself.

1

**ERYL MAI:** (Barely above a whisper)
But listen to me!
In my dream the school was enveloped in cloud,
black as coal.
Something...
(Noisily catching breath)
...**heavy**...
icy-cold, glistening wet
had slid
over my school.
(Emotionally)
And **all** the buildings **and** the school yard
had been swallowed-up;
with everybody still inside, Mammy!
But I...
was gliding-along
...above.
No longer using my feet.
Yet I had reached the entrance to the school.
Then...
I found myself to be in two places at once,
you see!
No! Not exactly that!
(Pause)
I felt a floating sensation.
And ...... saw my own body
buried deep underfoot...
entombed in wet slurry!
(Long pause)
...Me! Sat at my own desk in the classroom.
Peter and June to the side, same as always...
...our faces ashen grey, streaked black.
(Long Pause)
All dead.
Peter.
June.
Me.
Smothered to death.

*ERYL MAI RETURNS TO HER PLACE AT THE TABLE AND CALMLY
DRINKS FROM THE GLASS OF MILK*

(Calmly and gently) I'm not at all afraid, Mammy! I love you ... ...
and Da! (Smiling briefly) There's no more to be said.

*ERYL MAI TAKES A BITE OF TOAST*

# THE SURVIVING TWIN

**OCTOBER 21ST, 1966, ABERFAN LAY SHROUDED IN EARLY MORNING MIST. THE MIST FLOATED UP THE STEEP SIDES OF THE VALLEY, STREAMING OFF THE TOP OF THE HIGHEST COAL TIP WHICH REARED ABOVE THE MOUNTAIN RIDGE. THE SKY WAS CLEAREST BLUE. THERE WAS A SOUND LIKE THE DULL RATTLE OF RUNAWAY RAILWAY TRUCKS AND THE TIP CRASHED DOWN THE MOUNTAINSIDE WITH TERRIFYING POWER AND CLAIMED THE LIVES OF 128 SCHOOL CHILDREN.**

**EVVIE,** SCREAMS LOUDLY BEFORE RUSHING INTO VIEW. EVVIE IS DRESSED IN NIGHTCLOTHES AND HAS BARE FEET.

**EVVIE:**     (Cradling head)
Another nightmare!    ...Can't erase the images.
It was the last day before half-term.
Miss Morgan rang the handbell at precisely three minutes to nine.
And we went to our classroom;
because it was Friday there was no assembly in the hall.
(Pause) There was rumbling, thunder!
Someone screamed.
The windows went dark...
...and all the walls came down on top of us.
And the roof was falling in.
(With rising aggitation)
I was trapped to the neck...
...couldn't breath.    I was terrified.
(Shouting)
Don't leave me here!    Where's my sister?
(Pause)
Miss Morgan was crying and sobbing;
digging, tearing at debris!
I fainted, I suppose: eveything went black.
Where's my sister?
The fireman smiled and put his helmet over my head,
'Shut-eyes there's rubbish coming down.'
(Evvie screws eyes tightly shut)
Where is my sister?
They dug down little by little.
*EVVIE TURNS HEAD TO ONE SIDE AND SCREAMS LOUDLY*
That's my sister, bleeding from the mouth.
Dead!
'No, dear. It's a dolly!'
Said the fireman;  and threw a blanket over.
I was carried out a long while after that.
Ma was waiting outside.
'Evvie, have you seen your sister?'
(Tonelessly)
Yes.
'Did you talk to her?    No,Ma; she was still.
*EVVIE BOWS HEAD*

# THE HAIR PARLOUR

**FRAN LOVES TO ACCOMPANY AUNTIE LIL TO THE LOCAL CORNER
HAIRDRESSERS WHICH IS RULED OVER BY A DOMINANT PEROXIDED
CHARACTER WHO IS GREATLY RESPECTED BY THE SATISFIED CLIENTELE.**

*3 CHAIRS IN LINE SET AT AN ANGLE TO A SINGLE CHAIR STANDING A
DISTANCE APART, FRAN WANDERS ACROSS AIMLESSLY – CAUGHT UP IN THE
DAYDREAM WORLD OF AN IMAGINATIVE LONELY CHILD WHO SPENDS
CONSIDERABLE TIME IN THE ADULT WORLD.*

**FRAN:**    Auntie Lil has her hair dressed at Yvonnes'
it's not a shop:
it's an ordinary house from the outside.
But it has **'Yvonnes'**...

*FRAN SLOWS AND STOPS*

...in pink writing
above the front window.
And nylon candyfloss nets of pale pink
at the window;
to hide the clients from the street.
(Pause)
It's Auntie Lil's favourite and only outing;
**the** visit to the hair parlour.
(Conspiratorially)
And **my** favourite place, too!
(Pause)
It's full of old ladies with salt and pepper hair
or hair of fading blue.
There are frizzy grown-out perms and drooping sets.
All waiting... To-Be-Done.
And every head turns, every old lady smiles at me
when I walk in with my auntie.

*FRAN SMILES AND CLOSES EYES AND BREATHES DEEP DRAUGHTS
OF AIR*

Permanent waving lotion, setting lotion
and gluey lacquer squirting out of squeezy bottles
have used up all the air: but even **that** thick cloying
heady mix is pushed aside without effort
by the heavy waves of Yvonne's terribly expensive perfume
rolling across the salon.
(Pause)
Yvonne,

**FRAN:** (With awe)
Orders the customers about!
Like a **very strict** old-fashioned schoolmistress
bossing young children about
in no-nonsense fashion in a classroom.
(Smiling)
She calls Auntie Lil, Mrs Baker...
even though she's known her twenty years.
(Loudly)
'Lovely to see you, Mrs Baker.
You look well! Hang your coat up, take a magazine
and sit down. Irene will be with you shortly,
backwash, isn't it?'
And before Auntie Lil is given the chance to reply
her coat has been snatched away
and she's been handed a magazine
pulled into a gown
and pushed into a chair next to the basins...

*FRAN LOOKS OVER AT THE SINGLE CHAIR*

...and a clean smelling towel has been wrapped-and-tucked
around her neck by Irene, the stylist
in less time than it takes to blink.
(Looking around thoughtfully)
**All** the old ladies do as they are told,
and they **never** fidget.
Yvonne wouldn't put up with it!
(Pause)
Even her own hair doesn't dare to fidget.
It's bright yellow and stiff
and **always** looks exactly the same.
(Confidentially)
I have tried to see if there are any joins;
I'm sure, almost sure that it's a wig!
**I** think she takes it off and hangs it up at night!

*FRAN MOVES TOWARDS THE SINGLE CHAIR*
*AND TURNS TO AN AREA NEARBY*

Most of all I love to watch Yvonne 'Doing a perm'.
She runs a comb through Auntie Lil's wet hair.
There's hardly any hair to comb
but Yvonne finds little strands
and takes thin wisps
and wraps them tight in papers around pink rubber curlers.
(Laughing)
Auntie Lil looks like nothing on earth!

**FRAN:** And **exactly** like the person seated next to her.
Everybody looks the same.
(Pause)
They didn't when they came in!
Yvonne makes them feel it's right and proper
to look alike.
(Pause)

*FRAN TURNS AND LOOKS DOWN AT THE ROW OF CHAIRS*

Yvonne pushes clients under the dryers...
...one at a time.
(Shouting loudly)
'Don't forget now, if it gets too hot turn down the heat.'
And she marches off saying,
'If I hear one more word about her varicose veins
I shall pull them out for her personally, on the spot!'
(Smiling)
They can't hear a word when they're 'Under the dryer'.
'Irene! Comb-out Mrs Baker she's had long enough
under, she'll be fried!'

*FRAN DEFINES A WIDE SWEEPING MOVEMENT*

And Yvonne storms across the salon like a ship in full sail,
'If we don't get a move on you'll be here all night,
Irene!
We've another six perms booked in for today!'

*FRAN LOOKS BACK AT THE ROW OF CHAIRS*

Irene rescues Auntie Lil; and she's pulled out
from under the dryer with a beetroot-red face.
She's wearing a thick hairnet and a pair
of artificial ears and a pale pink nylon gown.
But that's the way they all look.
(Pause)
If I listen to the conversation its always
about doctors and the weather.
That's all old ladies talk about!
(Pause)
Auntie Lil is steered across the patterned vinyl
holding her handbag in one hand and the magazine
in the other.
She hasn't so much as flicked through the pages,
she never does!
(Pause)

**FRAN:**    Finally, Auntie Lil is combed-out by Yvonne personally.
They **all** are!
'That's what the client gets here, the personal touch!'
She reminds auntie, addressing her silent mirror image.
It remains for Auntie Lil to sit stiffly
and hold her breath
for a VERY long time under a cloud of laquer that settles
and glues the shocked hair in place.

*FRAN WALKS FORWARD*

Auntie Lil pays and tips
Yvonne licks a finger and flicks through an
appointment diary bigger than a Bible,
makes the next appointment for Tuesday week...
And reminds her that it's been hard to 'fit-her-in!
(Pause)
Auntie Lil is grateful...

*FRAN TURNS TO LEAVE*

...Her hair is too tightly curled; and face flushed.

*FRAN WALKS SLOWLY*

...But Auntie Lil is pleased with her hair-do.

*FRAN TURNS BACK*

She's had a **special** day-out.

# THE TAP DANCER

**CAMILLA IS BY NO MEANS AN EXPERIENCED TAP DANCER AND MIGHT HAVE HAD ONLY A SINGLE LESSON IN TAP. CAMILLA IS SELF ASSURED AND FASHION-AWARE, ASSERTIVE WITH AFFECTED MANNERISMS AND SHE IS ACCUSTOMED TO GETTING HER OWN WAY! SHE SEES A GLITTERING FUTURE FOR HERSELF – IN SHOWBUSINESS. (CAMILLA MIGHT SPEAK WITH A SOUTH LONDON OR REGIONAL ACCENT).**

***ENTER: CAMILLA,*** *NOISILY IN TAPSHOES, CONCEALING 'SOMETHING' BEHIND HER BACK. SHE CLATTERS FORWARD ANGRILY.*

**CAMILLA:**  Can't tap on carpet.
It's **impossible!**

*SHE TAPS A TOE AND POUTS*

And then...
If I don't practise...
(Pause)
Well! That'll be that.
I'll **never** make it to the top:
never see my name in lights.

*SHE ATTEMPTS A SHUFFLE, HOP, STEP*

Showbiz is **desperately** competitive, you know.

*SHE ADOPTS A PHOTOGRAPHIC STUDIO LONG-NECK POSE AND SIGHS IN EXAGGERATED FASHION*

Life's really not fair!

*SHE PULLS OUT A VASE IN TWO FRAGMENTS FROM BEHIND HER BACK AND VIEWS THE BREAKAGE WITH CONCERN*

(Sulkily)
I was only trying to perfect the routine, after all.

*SHE ATTEMPTS TO PIECE THE VASE TOGETHER*

Her favourite!
(Pause)
What am I going to say?
(Fast to herself)
Ttt, ttt, ttt, ttt...
Of course I know **now** that I shouldn'tve
been standing on top of the sideboard.
It **was** a silly thing to do...

*SHE SHAKES HER HEAD*

**CAMILLA:**   ...It just wasn't big enough to tap dance on!

*SHE SHUFFLES HER FEET AND SHRUGS HER SHOULDERS*

Actually, everything was fine...
...until I did the high kick!
Then the vase sort've, sprang up.
And flew through the air!
(Following the movement of the vase)
And landed in two pieces the other side of the room.

*SHE TAPS LOUDLY IN A TIGHT CIRCLE*

Could blame the cat!
(Pause)
Trouble with that is...
After the accident,
when I tried to stand the pieces up again
on the sideboard,
hoping it'd look as if nothing had happened.
**Then,** only when it was far too late:
did I notice lots and lots of little dug out pits
in the smooth wood, just where I'd been tapping.
She'll know the cat can't've done that!

*SHE HOLDS UP THE OFFENDING FRAGMENTS AND EVALUATES*

(Optimistically)
Perhaps the little pits won't be noticed.
Perhaps the vase won't be missed for ages and ages –
If I just keep quiet.

*SHE SMILES; THE SMILE GIVES WAY TO A LOOK OF HORROR*

What if she's given masses of flowers?
The'll be nothing to put them in!

*SHE PACES AND STAMPS A FOOT IN UTTER FRUSTRATION*

What am I going to do?
Suppose I'll have to own up and cry a lot.
That's all I can do.

*SHE TURNS CATCHING A SOUND AND HASTENS TO ONE SIDE.
SHE LISTENS OUT AND PULLS A FACE BEFORE RUSHING BACK*

She's on her way downstairs, **HELP!**

*SHE VIEWS THE FRAGMENTS WITH DESPERATION*

**CAMILLA:** (Shouting)
Mummy! There's something I want to talk to you about.

*SHE SEARCHES FOR SOMEWHERE TO HIDE THE BROKEN VASE FINALLY CLASPS THE FRAGMENTS BEHIND HER BACK IN PANIC*

Mummy! I want to give up tap... I hate it!

*SHE THROWS DOWN THE VASE ANGRILY AND STORMS OFF*

**EXIT CAMILLA.**

# CABBAGE

**SAM IS A NORMAL OUTGOING CHILD HOLDING POSITIVE VIEWS ON ALMOST EVERYTHING. SAM IS DRESSED IN WEEK-END CASUAL CLOTHING.**

***ENTER: SAM,*** *CLUTCHING A 'DUTCH' CABBAGE, ONE SHOELACE UNDONE. SAM WANDERS WITH LITTLE SENSE OF PURPOSE, HALTS ON NOTICING THE OFFENDING SHOELACE AND STOOPS, PUTTING DOWN THE CABBAGE, BEFORE TYING THE LACE CRUDELY AND RETRIEVING THE CABBAGE.*

**SAM:**     I was sent to buy it...

*SAM VIEWS THE CABBAGE HEAD WITH CAUTIOUS SUSPICION*

...It'd been forgotten.

*SAM VIEWS THE CABBAGE UNDERSIDE WITH EXTREME DISTASTE*

How could anyone forget?
(Pause)
Cost a fortune.

*SAM SHAKES HEAD GLUMLY, AN EXAGGERATED SIGH ESCAPES SAM MOVES CLOSER TO REVEAL A SECRET*

Boring, boring colour.

*SAM SNIFFS THE CABBAGE*

**Smelly!**
(Pause)
And massive; absolutely enormously huge!

*BOWING UNDER THE WEIGHT OF THE CABBAGE*

Phew! And hard as a rock.

*SAM ADOPTS A NEW STANCE, EXAMINES THE HEAD FROM A VARIETY OF ANGLES*

Cabbage.
**Yuk!**
(Pause)
Well!

*SAM HOLDS THE CABBAGE ALOFT*

**This!**
(Conspiritorially)
Requires SKILLED preparation.
**This!** Demands the attention of the longest
and sharpest of kitchen knives
to hack through and halve.

*SAM TUCKS CABBAGE UNDER AN ARM AND MIMES A STRENUOUS SAWING ACTION*

**SAM:** Eventually, knife will saw through to chopping board.
And, **that** will signal the start of the shredding process!
(Sigh)
Shredding will create a **mountain** of wormy slithers...
(With horror)
...Enough to fill a huge saucepan to the brim!
The saucepan lid will need to be forced down hard:
and cabbagy worms will squeak and squeal in protest
as they squeeze-up inside and make contact
with **boiling** water.

*SAM PAUSES, EYES WIDE FACE INCREDULOUS*

Then, in no time
a curling yellow stench will swirl
into every hidden corner of my house.
(Conspiratorially)
That's nothing!
That rotting stench is capable of filling
whole schools; and hospitals, too.
Quite easily, any day of the week!

*SAM TOYS WITH THE CABBAGE*

When. **THIS!** has been cooked.
(Pause)
When, the saucepan lid is gently lifted:
a miracle will have taken place.
The cabbage will have vanished!
(Pause)
Unfortunately, not completely.
But it will've shrunk beyond recognition.
And thin, lifeless silent cabbage-worms
will be swilling around in ditchwater
right at the bottom of the saucepan.

*SAM VIEWS THE CABBAGE WITH WONDER*

There's **always,** 'Just enough for everyone'.
**This!**
(Viewing the cabbage with dread)
Will appear as a straggling heap on my plate,
later today.
Then; as I fidget at table, avoiding it,
working around the unmentionable with the

**SAM:**     precise skill of a surgeon.
A voice will interrupt.
(Condescending tone)
'Eat up your cabbage, it's good for you!'

*SAM PULLS A FACE*

I don't think grown-ups always tell the truth.
Nothing that looks or smells that way can be good!

*SAM LOOKS OVER A SHOULDER, PLACES CABBAGE AT FEET*

(Shouting)
Over here.

*SAM PAUSES FOR UNHEARD REPLY*

I can play for a while.

*SAM PAUSES*
*SHRUGS SHOULDERS IN RESPONSE TO AN UNHEARD QUESTION*

No! I'm in no hurry.


*SAM PAUSES TO LISTEN TO A FURTHER UNHEARD QUESTION*

How about football?

*SAM SMILES AND DRIBBLES THE CABBAGE HEAD A SHORT
DISTANCE BEFORE KICKING THE CABBAGE OFF STAGE HARD.*

**EXIT SAM.**

# SOFIA

AT THE TURN OF THE CENTURY AN UNASSUMING POLISH WOMAN RECEIVED THE NOBEL PRIZE FOR PHYSICS AND ACHIEVED WORLD FAME AND RESPECT FOR DISCOVERIES ABOUT RADIATION THAT WOULD CHANGE THE COURSE OF HISTORY. MARIE (MANYA) CURIE PIONEERED A COMPLETELY NEW AREA OF SCIENCE AND OPENED UP THE FIELD OF SCIENTIFIC RESEARCH TO WOMEN AND HER BRILLIANT SCIENTIFIC ACHIEVEMENT WAS FUNDAMENTAL TO THE UNDERSTANDING OF THE ATOM - AND PROVIDED A REVOLUTIONARY TREATMENT FOR CANCER THAT IS IN USE TO THIS DAY.

*MANYA IS SLIGHTLY BUILT AND SERIOUS BUT THE QUIET SHYNESS MASKS TREMENDOUS INNER STRENGTH AND DETERMINATION. MANYA CARES LITTLE FOR FRILLS AND PREFERS SIMPLE DRESS AND WEARS HER HAIR LOOSE.*

***A SMALL TABLE AND CHAIR,*** *MANYA IS SEATED AND WRITES RAPIDLY. SHE PAUSES BRIEFLY TO REFER TO A TEXTBOOK BEFORE DIPPING PEN INTO INK BOTTLE AND CONTINUING TO WRITE. SHE BREAKS OFF, TO LOOK UPWARDS. HER EYES FOLLOWING A MOVEMENT ACROSS THE CEILING.*

**MANYA:**  Feet!
(Whispering)
You hear, sister?
(Pause)
**Feet,** Sofia.
Impatient young feet clatter across floorboards overhead.
You hear, dearest?

*MANYA TURNS TO THE SIDE AND LISTENS OUT*

Up, down staircases.
Feet of your exact foot size, and larger!

*MANYA BANGS THE TABLE TOP RHYTHMICALLY*

Pounding
up, down, up, down.
Like any day, Sofia.
(Pause)
Like, any other day.
(Pause)
You hear shrieks... chatter... bustle?

*MANYA CRADLES HER HEAD IN HER HANDS, SHAKES HER HEAD*

...Laughter?
Hark! Sofia.
(Pause)
La-da, da-da, da-da.
Can you hear girls struggle to learn?

**MANYA:** (Pause)
Why so hard for them to learn? Eh?
(Pause)
And what of poor Mamma, older-looking, even more exhausted?
With family squeezed into these few rooms on the second,
like filling in a sandwich,
boarding school above and below...
(Pause)
Mama hasn't the strength necessary to run school
even with Papa to help.
(She sighs)
A terrible black cloud hangs over my home, Sofia.
A terrible black cloud.
What will become of us?

*MANYA PICKS UP THE TEXTBOOK*

But your little Manya learns, Sofia.
Even today.
You want that?

*MANYA SMILES AND NODS IN AFFIRMATIVE AND CLASPS THE
BOOK TIGHT TO HER BODY*

I **will** have culture and knowledge;
**will** use my mind to be useful in the world one day.
As Mamma and Papa wish...
...As you would have wished.

*MANYA OPENS THE BOOK AND RUNS A FINGER OVER TEXT*

Logic, Sofia; this alone remains constant.

*MANYA CAREFULLY LAYS DOWN THE BOOK, STANDS AND
PUSHES BACK THE CHAIR, THE CHAIRLEGS SCRAPE NOISILY*

(Whispering)
Let me take a peep inside the polished glass case.

*MANYA MOVES SLOWLY FROM THE TABLE*

(Sighing)
Dearest Sofia Sklodowska,
when I woke at dawn it was cold as yesterday...
...cold as death. And night-time tears had
crystallized and hung as frost patterns at the window.

*MANYA TOUCHES HER FACE*

**MANYA:** There were no more tears to be shed.
I knew you would not be the one to shake me awake.
**Knew** you would not be here to help Mamma wrap Bronya, Hela,
Joseph and me, your little Manya against the
bitter January cold.
If the five Sklodowska children could have
crunched through snowy cobbled streets, today.
If you could have led us through Old Warsaw...
...to climb the battlements and look out at
the frozen Vistula... if only.

*MANYA STANDS ON TIPTOE TO PEER INTO THE IMAGINARY CASE*

What orderly strange collection lies inside
the polished case belonging to Papa.
Shining glass tubes, bottles... in line.
Tiny dishes, precise scales.
(defining small delicate shapes with fingers)
Rock samples
(Pause)
and a mysterious machine.
Physics apparatus...
...order, Sofia.
...Logic.

*MANYA CROSSES BACK TO THE TABLE*

(Quietly)
First one pupil, then another fell ill:
One here, One there ...... no logic.
Then you and Bronya.
**Typhus:** for weeks your bodies burned.
(Pause)
Slowly, slowly Bronya grew better...
**recovered.**

*MANYA SITS AT THE TABLE*

But **you!**
You failed to recover, Sofia Sklodowska.
(Long pause)
Yesterday, Wednesday I saw you for the last time.
(Calling loudly)
Dearest sister, you hear me?
Hear anything? Sofia?

*MANYA SHAKES HER HEAD GRAVELY, PICKS UP THE PEN AND
LOOSES HERSELF IN WORK*

16

# GOODBYE MOTHER GOOSE

**BRYONY IS FASCINATED BY THEATRE AND BELIEVES IN THE ENCHANTING FANTASY WORLD OF PANTOMIME AND HAS NO WISH TO DISPEL ILLUSION; YET IS ANXIOUS TO DISCOVER ITS SECRETS AND TO LEARN ABOUT THE DECEPTIONS EMPLOYED WHEN AN OPPORTUNITY ARISES FOR HER TO MEET PRISCILLA, THE PANTOMIME GOOSE, BACKSTAGE – AFTER A PERFORMANCE.**

*ENTER: BRYONY, RUSHING FORWARD, CLUTCHING A DOWNY WHITE FEATHER. BRYONY IS DRESSED FOR THE THEATRE AND BUBBLING WITH EXCITEMENT, DESPERATE TO RELATE EVENTS AND STRIVING TO CONVEY THE SPECIAL NATURE OF HER EXPERIENCE TO HER OLDER SISTER (THE UNSEEN SISTER IS STANDING DIRECTLY IN FRONT OF BRYONY).*

**BRYONY:**     Guess what?

*SHE PAUSES BRIEFLY FOR AN UNHEARD RESPONSE*

After the panto I went backstage...
...To meet the goose.
The **real** one!
(Pause)
And she told me all her secrets.

*SHE LOOKS SMUG AND SWINGS HER SKIRT FROM SIDE TO SIDE*

She **did!**
(Pause)
Like, there **were** other gooses around
but Priscilla lay huge gold eggs **so**
(Stretching out the word with outstretched arms)
b..e..a..u..t..ifully
that Mother Goose always, but always,
insisted on having **her** as only friend-in-the-world.
Anyway, all the others were pale imitations:
Priscilla had trod the boards for over half a century!

*SHE LISTENS TO AN UNHEARD COMMENT*

Of course I knew there was a person inside!
Everybody knows that!
Well! This **was** the person.
And she wasn't much taller than me...
...Tiny, like a bird; a little sparrow.
Not at all like an old lady.

*SHE TAKES IN A REMARK WHILST STROKING THE FEATHER*

**BRYONY:** (With agitation)
I did! I did see the goose!
(Pointing to the side)
The goose was propped-up against the corner
without anybody inside.
And the yellow legs were saggy
with wrinkles where knees had been.
And big flat birdfeet joined on to the legs.
(Thoughtfully)
The feet were standing close-together
like a pair of wellingtons waiting
to be stepped into.
(With disappointment)
But...
...Close-to the old goose looked dirty and dead-looking...
not the same, at all.

*SHE PAUSES TO TAKE IN A REMARK*

Well! What really **was** weird about the whole thing
was that there were just the two of us
in the dressing room...
...But the tiny lady spoke as if there were three:
as if the goose **was** alive.

*SHE PAUSES BRIEFLY FOR AN UNHEARD COMMENT*

(Slowly and carefully)
No! She was not a loony!
Priscilla was her special best friend, that's all.

*SHE LOOKS DOWN AT THE FEATHER AFFECTIONATELY*

She gave it to me...
...Loose feathers were everywhere.

*SHE REMAINS PENSIVE FOR A MOMENT BEFORE BUBBLING UP*

Do you know? Priscilla used to fly across the stage every night...
...High-up in the air, in a sky filled with
twinkling stars and a glittering paper moon.
She flew for years and years.
But **then**...
(A dramatic pause)
...Something went very wrong.
And she fell from the sky.

*SHE SHRUGS AND GRIMACES IN RESPONSE TO AN UNHEARD
COMMENT*

**BRYONY:** Have it **your** way!
She didn't fall.
She was dropped; and landed in the orchestra pit.
(Pause)
**Well!** She never forgave the boy for dropping her
and refused to fly ever again after that.
That's not **all** she told me, either.
The lady actually made Priscilla herself:
glued on every feather one at a time.
What do you think of **that?**

*SHE LOOKS ENQUIRINGLY BEFORE SHAKING HER HEAD IN*
*NEGATIVE REPLY*

The lady had made six goose-skins altogether
over the years... she showed me old photos.
The all looked the same to me...
but she could tell the difference.
(Pause)
Priscilla was her favourite from the start though.

*SHE LISTENS TO A FURTHER UNHEARD QUESTION*

She considered the face... more appealing;
**and** the feathers were top-grade.
(Knowledgeably)
It didn't end with the making either;
there was always work to be done.

*SHE LISTENS IMPATIENTLY TO AN UNHEARD QUESTION*

Repairing!
I told you feathers kept falling off...

*SHE THRUSTS THE FEATHER FOWARD TO PUSH THE POINT*

...Priscilla's delicate.

*SHE HOLDS HER ARMS TIGHTLY TO HER SIDES AND THRUSTS HER*
*HEAD FOWARD AND CONCENTRATES HARD AS SHE WADDLES A*
*FEW STEPS ON OUT-TURNED FEET.*

*SHE SPINS AROUND.*

What's so funny?
There's a **lot** more to it than you think!
SHE practised for hours and hours
in front of a long mirror before she even considered
being a goose.
**Actually,** I think I might like to be a pantomime
goose when **I** grow up!

*SHE PAUSES BEFORE RESPONDING TO AN UNHEARD FINAL
QUESTION BY DEFINING A SMALL SQUARE SHAPE IN FRONT OF
HER EYES*

**BRYONY:**  ...At the bottom of the goose's neck.
But you can only just-about see where you are going.
Can't look up or down or to the side.
Can't use your arms to balance...
...and the feet are easy to trip-over.
She said, if you fall down
you can't get up again.
Two people have to lift you!
Would **you** like to be left lying on your back
kicking your legs in the air out in the middle of the stage?
It had happened to her; someone moved a prop.
She never forgave **that** boy either.


*SHE PLACES THE FEATHER ON A PALM AND BLOWS GENTLY THEN
TRAPS THE FLOATING FEATHER BETWEEN CUPPED HANDS*


When it was time to say goodbye
the tiny lady told me that we wouldn't meet again.
(Pause)
They were going to live in the country.
Town life no longer suited old Priscilla.
(Pause)
She pulled herself up from the chair
and made her way over to the corner
and stroked Priscilla's neck.
(Pause)
And I did the same... but I hardly dared to touch,
it was falling to pieces with age.
I'm sure she knew that I was thinking that the goose
couldn't last another season...
(Pause)
...Didn't know what to say.
...She kissed me goodbye.
I, ...didn't know what to say.
I thought back to the shrieks of laughter that had
greeted Priscilla's every entrance; the countless
wishes for her happiness as she passed through
the enchanted pantomime-world.
(Pause)

**BRYONY:** So, I couldn't help feeling sad as I looked back
at the bird-like old lady standing with her hand
resting gently on the tired-looking neck
of her only friend.

*HER SMILE IS DIRECTED AT THE FEATHER AS SHE TURNS TO WALK
AWAY*

I shall think of her before I go to sleep;
sharing her memories with Priscilla...
...in the country.

**EXIT BRYONY.**

# THE DINNER PARTY GUEST

**CHLOE IS A PRIVILEGED CHILD FROM A WELL-TO-DO FAMILY AND HER PARENTS FREQUENTLY ENTERTAIN ON A LAVISH SCALE. CHLOE IS FASCINATED BY ONE PARTICULAR REGULAR DINNER GUEST AND MAKES A POINT OF CREEPING OUT FROM HER BEDROOM AND HIDING ON THE LANDING IN ORDER TO CATCH GLIMPSES OF THE OLD ECCENTRIC WHENEVER SHE VISITS.**

***ENTER: CHLOE,*** *BAREFOOTED AND DRESSED FOR BED, CREEPING STEALTHILY ON TIPTOE.*

**CHLOE:**    (Whispering)
Violet Abercrombie's on her way at last.
She phoned to say she couldn't find a taxi
for love nor money, what in Heaven's name
was Finchley coming to?
So she's being collected.
(Pause)
Violet Abercrombie's...
**...extraordinary!**

*SHE STANDS DREAMILY*

There can't be anyone else like her
anywhere in the whole wide world!
(Pause)
Even her name's especially special.
(Savouring syllables)
Vio / let / Aber / crom / bie.
She's **ancient...** and because of that
she powders over her deep-wrinkled face
with palest face powder;
and wears circles of heavy rouge on her cheeks
rather like a pantomime dame.

*SHE CASTS AN EYE OVER HER HANDS*

Her hands are gnarled...
...and incredibly old-looking
with long, long scarlet finger nails
and lipstick to match.
And she wears all of her flaming red hair
piled high on her head: it must be dyed! I suppose.
(With fascination)
And Violet Abercrombie smokes cigars after dinner
even though she's a lady.

*SHE DEMONSTRATED THE AFFECTED MANNER IN WHICH A CIGAR*
*IS HELD BETWEEN THUMB AND FINGER*
*AND MIMES THE PLEASURABLE EXHALATION OF SMOKE*

**CHLOE:** (Smiling)
She wears a long black velvet gown, **always.**
I've never seen her in anything different.
(Confidentially)
She uses a Simplicity pattern.
Runs-up gowns herself,
every new one exactly identical to the last!
(Pause for conjecture)
Her house must be filled with black velvet:
a whole house full of black gowns... imagine!
(Pause)
**But,**
curiously, she is known to use only the one handbag.
She carries that gianormous battered old bag
on her arm and **won't** be parted from it
for a single moment...
...to look at her it's possible to believe
that the handbag has been glued to her person.

*SHE DISPLAYS SIGNS OF IMPATIENCE*

Where is she?
She should've been here by now!

*SHE SWEEPS FORWARD AGGRESSIVELY IN THE MANNER OF A*
*GRAND ENTRANCE*

No need to look down; I know she cant've arrived
for her arrivals are noisy affairs.
She billows in like a ship in full sail
and her voice reaches my bedroom long before
she's had time to step through the front door.

*SHE CREEPS FOWARD TO THE VERY EDGE OF THE STAGE*

(Whispering)
And when I hear her voice
I creep from my bedroom and quietly cross the landing.

*SHE SMILES FONDLY AND UNHURRIEDLY*

But there's something **far** more special about her
than strong voice and violent hair.
(Pause)
Violet Abercrombie wears **real** jewels.
That's why I hide on the landing whenever she's
invited; I love to see her jewels.

*SHE KNEELS AND PEERS BELOW*

At the last dinner party I waited ages before
catching my first glimpse of her in the hallway below.
(Pause)
She had spent longer than usual dismissing the
taxi driver and offering explanations for her lateness.
Then, I caught sight of her.
Her diamond earrings swung like chandeliers,
a diamond necklace fell like a waterfall from
her throat...
...and she was wearing wide bracelets
and rings, there were several rings.
All ...**matched.**
A whole matching set of
shimmering diamonds...
...A million stars suspended in a black
velvety sky...
(Pause)
If those jewels were not hers...
...they'd belong to the Queen!
That's obvious.

*SHE STANDS*

That last time: she swept through hurridly.
All too soon the diamonds had disappeared from view.
And Violet Abercrombie had joined the others
in the dining room.
(Pause)
And I hid on the landing: mumbles and shrieks
of grown-up laughter drifted up to me in bursts
as I waited.
(Pause)
At last...
...the dining room door opened.

*SHE KNEELS*

Violet Abercrombie passed underneath leaving me
to play the guessing game.
She was smiling to herself and I knew that
she had a trick up her sleeve.
The clatter of plates signalled a break between course
as Violet Abercrombie made her way back
from the cloakroom.

*SHE LEANS FORWARD*

**CHOLE:** Her red hair was vibrant and intensely red...
...redder!
For she had changed her jewels
and now wore rubies.
A complete set.

The diamonds had been neatly boxed and now lay
with her other sets back inside the handbag.
(Pause)
The wait between main course and dessert was unbearable.
But eventually she emerged again
and rubies were exchanged for emeralds.
And then, something extraordinary.
She caught sight of me as she passed beneath.
She smiled and waved.
Magical light burst from
a stone in her ring
like a shooting star!
I made a wish.

*SHE STANDS*

This is no ordinary person!
I told myself.
(Pause)
This is my fairy godmother.
And I looked at her in a new light.
(Pause)
And to think I'd always been a little afraid of her.

*SHE CATCHES A SOUND AND REACTS WITH EXCITEMENT AND
KNEELS QUICKLY*

(Whispering)
She's arrived at last, I can hear her voice.
Violet Abercrombie...

*SHE TOUCHES HER THROAT AND EAR LOBES*

...will you be wearing your diamonds tonight?

*CHLOE PEERS DOWN*

# NINE LIVES

**ZED IS ATTEMPTING TO COME TO TERMS WITH THE DEATH OF THE FAMILY CAT. ZED IS SEATED AT A SMALL TABLE FRONT STAGE, USING A SQUEAKY FELT MARKER TO COMPLETE A NOTICE. ZED STANDS, THE CHAIRLEGS SCRAPE NOISILY**

**ZED:** (Sadly)
Tisis went to the vet yesterday,
to have his claws clipped.
(Pause)
And never came back.
(Reading the notice)
'IN AFFECTIONATE REMEMBRANCE OF TISIS
MY CAT... BORN
(Sighing)
...A LONG WHILE AGO.'
A little vague
(Shrugging)
but there you go!
(Confidentially)
Haven't a clue how old he was!
He wandered in from nowhere,
a grown-up stray with a torn ear.
So long ago that I hadn't even been born!
(Pensively)
Tisis must've been incredibly old, though!
Because his tail had grown thin and stringy.
(Smiling)
Not that I loved him any the less for that!
(Long pause)
The vet told us that Tisis was worn-out.
And appeared confused!
**Huh!**
Only goes to show that the vet didn't
know much about anything!
Or he would've realised that poor-old Tisis
wasn't so much confused as 'not-terribly-bright'.
(Confidentially)
Come to think of it that's probably
why he got lost in the first place.

*ZED RUSHES BACK TO THE TABLE AND MAKES RAPID ALTERATIONS TO THE NOTICE*

(Reading the notice)
'IN AFFECTIONATE REMEMBRANCE OF TISIS, MY CAT WHO ENJOYED NINE LONG AND HAPPY LIVES.'

*ZED SMILES AND WALKS OFF*

**EXIT ZED**

# TO GET THE GOAT

**CHARLIE BOY/GIRL LOVES TO RECEIVE BUT IF ANY GIFT SHOULD FAIL TO LIVE UP TO EXPECTATION IS UNGRACIOUS IN THE EXTREME - REGARDING AN OBLIGATORY 'THANK-YOU' PHONECALL AS A FINAL INSULT.**

*A TELEPHONE SITS IN PROMINENT POSITION ON SMALL TABLETOP WITH CRUMPLED GIFTWRAP AND RIBBON LYING NEARBY ON THE FLOOR. CHARLIE BOY/GIRL LIES SPRAWLED ACROSS AN ADJACENT EASY CHAIR EXAMINING A LEATHER WALLET WITHOUT ENTHUSIASM.*

**CHARLIE BOY**  (Eyeing wallet disparagingly)
(or)  Didn't want a leather wallet:
**CHARLIE GIRL:**  (Sitting up)
didn't ask for one.
It should've been blatantly obvious that
it's not much've a present to receive.
Why didn't anyone think
to ask me in the first place?
...IF I'dve had a say in the matter
I could've said,
(Sweetly)
Please, please may I have MONEY...
...or
a cheque would-do-nicely thank you
so I might choose for myself, you understand.
(Smelling the leather)
Poof!
Honestly, I'd rather've had
thank-you notelets
and **that's** saying something!
At least notelets would've smelled sweeter.
(Smelling the leather)
POOF!
That's the worst've it!
It smells FOUL!

*CHARLIE BOY/GIRL PULLS A FACE ON GINGERLY OPENING UP THE WALLET*

**No wonder!**
GOATSKIN!...
...EEER!
Says here...
(Reading with exaggeration)
Levant Goat.

*CHARLIE BOY/GIRL PUZZLES OVER THE OFFENDING WORDING*

**CHARLIE BOY/**  So, what's a Levant goat when it's at home?
**CHARLIE GIRL:**  (Gasping with horror)
New-born?
Or...
(Shrugging and grimacing)
...Wild mountain variety?
(Pause for thought)
Got it!
Smelliest cud-chewer in the entire galaxy,
MMM, that's a pretty fair description
of a Levant! I'd say.

*CHARLIE BOY/GIRL SCOWLS AT THE TELEPHONE*

I aught to phone
to say 'Thank-you-very-much'
but I don't want to!
Why should I?
It's not **fair**
no one elses relatives give
horrible smelly pressies.

*CHARLIE BOY/GIRL MOVES FROM THE CHAIR AND LIFTS THE
TELEPHONE RECEIVER RELUCTANTLY*

(Sighing loudly while dialling)
Time to lie through my teeth.
(Sweetly)
Hello?
It's me! Charlie Boy/Girl.
(Pulling a face)
Oh!   A wallet's always useful.
Special, yes!
(Over enthusiastically)
**Very** smart and grown-up......
(Pulling a face)
......Thank you SO much
(Flipping open the wallet)
for the wonderful Levant goat wallet.
Actually, what is a Levant goat?

*CHARLIE BOY/GIRL REGISTERS SURPRISE AT THE EXPLANATION
OFFERED*

**CHARLIE BOY/**   Mmmm.  Well I never!
**CHARLIE GIRL:**   (Pause)
              Hadn't a **clue**;
              thought it might've referred to size or something.
              Why not simply say 'Moroccan goat'?
              (Pause)
              The wallet wasn't made in Morocco!
              (Pause)
              How confusing.
              ...Irregular creases. Yes!
              ...Style of leather, Moroccan style.
              **Now** I understand.
              (Pause)
              No! I haven't.

*CHARLIE BOY/GIRL RESTS THE RECEIVER ON THE TABLE OPENS
UP THE WALLET COMPLETELY AND DRAWS OUT A CHEQUE.
CHARLIE BOY/GIRL THROWS DOWN THE WALLET AND GAZES
AT THE CHEQUE*

*CHARLIE BOY/GIRL BEAMS WITH DELIGHT BEFORE SNATCHING
UP THE RECEIVER*

              OH! ...OH!
              **Thank** you for the cheque...
              ...Ah!
              And for the beautiful Moroccan style
              leather wallet, of course.

*CHARLIE BOY/GIRL SLAPS DOWN THE TELEPHONE RECEIVER,
KISSES THE CHEQUE, SNATCHES UP THE WALLET AND SKIPS
OFF WAVING THE CHEQUE HIGH IN THE AIR.*

              **WOW!**

                                      **EXIT CHARLIE BOY/GIRL**

# THE GROCER'S

**IN THE NINETEEN TWENTIES SHOPKEEPERS WORKED HARD TO PROVIDE EXCELLENT SERVICE FOR THE UPPER AND MIDDLE CLASS CUSTOMERS AND UNHURRIED PERSONAL ATTENTION WAS PROVIDED BY BAKER, GREENGROCER, MILKMAN AND GROCER ALIKE.**

*A LOW EASY CHAIR WITH ARMS, CONNIE STANDS A DISTANCE BEHIND AND WALKS FORWARD AND AROUND TO THE SIDE OF THE CHAIR WITHOUT ONCE TAKING EYES OFF IT. CONNIE IS SUBDUED AND PENSIVE AND OF NEAT TIDY APPEARANCE EXCEPT FOR MUDDY SHOES AND MUD SPLATTERED LEGS. CONNIE STANDS AND STARES FOR A MOMENT BEFORE ADDRESSING THE CHAIR.*

**CONNIE:**   I shall never walk down the road again...

*CONNIE TURNS FROM THE CHAIR*

I feel too ashamed.
(Pause)
It **began** as an ordinary day
with Mother telephoning the grocer's first thing.
to give the weekly order.
(Pause)
She carefully ticked off every item
as she read out the list, as she always does.
And there's never a mistake.

*CONNIE WALKS FORWARD AND LOOKS INTO THE MIDDLE DISTANCE*

It was after the delivery boy on the bike
had staggered up to the house with a boxful
and left:
that Mother asked me to help unpack.
(Pause)
As the box grew more and more empty Mother's 'nagging doubt's'
grew too! At last the box was completely empty...
...no butter!
Mother reached for her list
and shook her head in disbelief.
Of course Reeves hadn't forgotten to send butter;
how silly of her to imagine that!
How could she have missed writing it on her list?

*CONNIE WANDERS ACROSS*

So Mother sent me on an errand to the grocer's.
(Pause)
It had rained heavily, earlier;

**CONNIE:**   ...and the road was muddy and a chain of puddles
lay along the path between my front gates
and Pescot Street.
I ran all the way, jumping puddles...

*CONNIE LOOKS DOWN AT SHOES AND LEGS*

...Even the biggest and deepest!
There was a long queue in Reeves
stretching back almost to the door.
(A sigh)
Knew it would take an age to be served
and took my place behind Mrs Padwick and the
usherette from the flea-pit who were standing
heads together whispering so loudly
that no one could fail to catch the tittle-tattle
as Mother calls it.

*CONNIE STANDS VERY STIFFLY AND CORRECTLY*

I counted green and brown patterned border tiles
that surrounded gleaming heavy-cream glazed squares
on the back wall...

*CONNIE POINTS A FINGER AND DEFINES THE SHAPE*

...behind the high counter...
(Shrinking small)
...hoping that I shouldn't be noticed
by the loose-tongued Mrs Padwick.
The long hand of the mahogany clock shuddered upwards:
and I grew bored.

*CONNIE STEPS FORWARD AND SMILES*

At **last!**

*CONNIE STANDS ON TIPTOE AND PEERS UPWARDS*

Pound of butter, please.
(Pause)
'Your mother forgot the butter, then?
Fancy, forgetting butter of all things.'

*CONNIE NODS IN AGREEMENT*

The girl chatted on in good-humoured fashion
as I watched her peel a slice from the slab.
I watched her pat the butter into shape
and slide it onto a square of white greaseproof.
I watched carefully as she placed it on the scales.

**CONNIE:**  One pound, exactly; not a fraction over... or under.
(Pause)
The greaseproof was... carefully folded,
then...
...An outer layer of brown paper, wrapped and
secured with carefully knotted string
with a loop for carrying.
(Smiling)
The Manager opened the door and wished me
'A good day'...
...And I swept out swinging the parcel.

*CONNIE SWINGS AN IMAGINARY PARCEL HIGH IN THE AIR*

I had tired of jumping puddles...

*CONNIE SWINGS THE IMAGINARY PARCEL AND HOP-SCOTCH
JUMPS WITH LEGS WIDE APART*

...tried to hop-scotch over every puddle
all the way home, without missing one!
But when I reached the massive puddle by the bridge...

*CONNIE'S HAND FLIES UP*

...The butter shot out of my hand!
At first I couldn't imagine where it had gone.
I searched around...
...and finally discovered the brown package
lying in the muddy road!
(Pause)
I picked it up gingerly.

*CONNIE STARES DOWN WITH GRAVE CONCERN*

I **daren't** arrive home with **that!**
So I unwrapped the butter.
(Guiltily)
I stuffed the muddy, wet brown paper
**and** the string
down the grating of a drain...
...and carried the butter home on my hand
in the thin white paper.

*CONNIE BREEZES FORWARD*

'Home, Mother.
Butter's on the table!'

*CONNIE RUNS AND SINKS GUILTILY IN THE CHAIR
AND STARES INTO AN IMAGINARY GRATE*

**CONNIE:** I stared into the fire without really watching
the dancing flames and held my breath...
...and waited.
(Long pause)
I heard Mother gasp.
I heard my name being called.
Mother asked if Reeves had given me the butter
**like that!**
(Guiltily)
'Yes!'
Before I had a chance to say another word
she was on the phone to Reeves;
she was demanding to speak to the manager!
(Pause)
I hadn't moved from the chair
when I heard a ring at the back door.

*CONNIE CLASPS THE ARMS OF THE CHAIR*
*HALF RISING FROM THE CHAIR BEFORE SINKING BACK*

**The manager!**
Reeves manager had come round to the house!

*CONNIE LOOKS UP*

He stood over me...
...'You know very well that the butter was
parcelled-up properly for you, don't you?'
(Pause)
I couldn't manage a word of reply,
I felt too ashamed.

*CONNIE HANGS HEAD IN SHAME.*

# THE CHILDREN'S HOUSE

SCHOOL USED TO BE UNIVERSALLY HATED BY PUPILS. AT THE TURN OF THE CENTURY NO ONE BELIEVED THAT ATTENDING SCHOOL COULD, OR SHOULD BE ENJOYABLE OR INTERESTING. A STRICT, REGIMENTED APPROACH WAS CONSIDERED VITAL AND UNQUESTIONING OBEDIENCE WAS DEMANDED OF PUPILS WORLDWIDE. MARIA MONTESSORI BECAME THE FIRST WOMAN DOCTOR IN ITALY AND SHE DEVISED METHODS OF TEACHING HANDICAPPED CHILDREN; SUCCESS LED TO AN OPPORTUNITY FOR HER TO APPLY THESE TO NORMAL CHILDREN. SHE OPENED A 'CHILDREN'S HOUSE' ON JANUARY 6, 1907 IN A SLUM DISTRICT OF ROME: A WORLD-WIDE PROGRESSION IN EDUCATION HAD BEGUN, WITH THE TRANSFORMATION OF THE CLASSROOM INTO AN EXCITING PLACE WHERE CHILDREN ARE THOUGHT OF AS PEOPLE.

*AN ORANGE BOX OR SMALL CRATE CENTRE STAGE, NONA WANDERS INTO VIEW, SHE IS CLEAN AND TIDY AND WEARS SIMPLE DRESS AND STURDY FOOTWEAR. SHE HOLDS A COLOURFUL GERBERA (or similar daisylike flower). NONA USES HER WHOLE BODY EXPRESSIVELY AND SHE IS LOOKING AT THE FLOWER BEFORE CATCHING SIGHT OF AN IMAGINED FRIEND.*

**NONA:**    (Calling)
Roberto...
(Waving and smiling)
**...Roberto!**
Do you want to walk with me to the Casa dei Bambini?

*PAUSE FOR UNHEARD REPLY*

In that case, shall I wait for you here?

*PAUSE FOR UNHEARD RESPONSE*

Hurry up, then!
We don't want to be late.

*NONA TURNS IDLY AND SMILES TO HERSELF PENSIVELY*

How everything has changed.
Before: none of us dreamt of a world outside...
...of a place to call our own.
Something like that would have been...
(Touching the air)
...beyond reach.
Beyond any dream.
(Pause)
We had few dreams, then.
We used to shamble around San Lorenzo...
(Head bowed)
...dull bewildered eyes staring blindly.
As if none of us had ever seen, or could see.
(Pause)

**NONA:** Prisoners, without hope.
There was poverty, misery, pain, fear.
And hunger.
Nothing more; that's all we could see.

*SHE RAISES HER ARMS HIGH ABOVE HER HEAD*

And if we were to look.
Tall, tall apartment blocks,
ugly and grey and squeezed too close.
Overcrowded squalid tenements.

*SHE WALKS A FEW PACES*

And the washing!
(Pause)
Lines of washing hanging from the fifth down
to the first floor,
stretching across each narrow alley
from one dark tumbledown slum-dwelling to the next.
Lines and lines of washing,
shutting out the sunlight.
(Pause)
But the washing couldn't muffle screaming arguments
and fights, no!
The washing never hid the violence.

*SHE MOVES OVER TO THE ORANGE BOX AND SITS*

Every wall in San Lorenzo had been kicked
and **kicked again.**
Every wall had been deliberately scratched and scarred.
Anything and everything that could be broken...
...broken.

*SHE KICKS HER HEELS AGAINST THE BOX*

Because we were shut out of our homes,
left to wander the streets until late in the evening.
(Pause)
I am not going to work in a factory when I am older!
Live out my life in San Lorenzo. **NO!**

*SHE SHAKES HER HEAD*

And nor is Roberto!
We shan't ever forget the humiliation we suffered
when the authorities used to, 'come-in'
from outside, to...
'de-louse the scugnizzi', the lousy 'ragazzo di strada'.
(Pause)
And we didn't even understand
that we were unhappy!

*SHE SMELLS THE FLOWER*

**NONA:**  Then...
...One morning, we were all collected up like stray dogs.
I was very frightened, but refused to show it.
Roberto was tearful.
We were bewildered; didn't know what was
going to happen.
Were we to be punished?
Taken away to the workhouse?
(Pause)
Outsiders took away all our clothes.
We were pushed into stiff blue smocks...
(Quietly)
...Of the kind given to, workhouse children.
(Pause)
We were **instructed** to hold hands.
An outsider tugged the arm of little Giuseppe,
who was first in line...
(Smiling)
...and we all had to follow, like the washing
on the pulley lines!

*SHE PUTS DOWN THE FLOWER*

We found ourselves in a room.
Oh! The sniffing and crying was pitiful.
I held Roberto's hand and he stopped crying
after a while.
And who should be standing in the centre of the room? Why!
None other than Signorina Nuccitelli,
daughter of the caretaker.
The Signorina looked considerably changed.
So clean and tidy in a new dress that I hardly recognised her:
I had never seen her look that way.

*SHE TOUCHES THE PETALS OF THE FLOWER*

And beside the Signorina: stood **an angel!**
This angel had stepped from a beautiful painting
hanging in the Cathedral...
(Crossing herself)
...Or so I believed!
Golden hair curled around her face and
**she** was wearing a new dress, **too!**

*SHE STANDS AND STEPS FORWARD AS IF TO GREET*

'My name is Doctor Montessori
Welcome to the Casa dei Bambini'.

**NONA:** Casa dei Bambini — children's house!
Doctor? A lady doctor?
Was that possible? No! A doctor is a man.

*SHE SHRUGS*

I was unable to make sense of that
but I could see that she was very kind.
We all saw that and there was no more crying.

*SHE MOVES AROUND LOOKING AT SPECIFIC PLACES*

Then I noticed small tables and chairs.
A chair for everyone!
There were no scratches;
**everything** was new and clean.
(Pause)
Doctor Montessori opened the doors of a tall cupboard.
And there lay bright shining playthings
in neat rows, on every shelf.
Roberto looked at me, and smiled
but we both felt too shy to play with anything
for a little while.
(Pause)
Doctor Montessori was watching us
and making notes in a book.
But I found something
that I liked to do and forgot all about her.

*SHE RETURNS TO THE ORANGE BOX AND PICKS UP THE FLOWER
BEFORE SITTING*

A bright place,
far removed from the stench and ugliness
that is San Lorenzo...
**...existed!**
(Pause)

*SHE TURNS TO ONE SIDE AND LISTENS OUT*

Roberto?
(Pause)
Is that you, Roberto?

*PAUSE FOR A RESPONSE*

I'll catch you up!

*SHE IMMEDIATELY STANDS AND MOVES PURPOSEFULLY IN THAT
DIRECTION*

I'm on my way.

**EXIT NONA**

# THE PIED PIPER

**HAMELIN, A PICTURE-BOOK MEDIEVAL GERMAN TOWN STANDS WITH A FAST FLOWING RIVER TO ONE SIDE AND RUGGED MOUNTAIN RANGE BEHIND.**

*A HALF-BARREL OR 3 LEGGED WOODEN STOOL CENTRE STAGE, THE LAME CHILD STANDS A DISTANCE AWAY LEANING HEAVILY ON A CRUDE HOME-MADE CRUTCH. THE PALE LAME CHILD IS DRESSED ENTIRELY IN BLACK WITH A LONG SCARF LOOSE AROUND THE NECK AND WEARS 'SURGICAL' BOOTS.*

**LAME**    No birdsong... laughter.
**CHILD:**   No!
Only mothers weeping for lost children;
and tight-lipped fathers hiding terrible anger.
And me, the one remaining child.
(Regretfully)
For I was left behind.

*THE LAME CHILD HOBBLES FOWARD DRAGGING THE CLUB-FOOT*

At one time the cobbled streets
were filled with children.
(Pause)
But this was to change...
Hamelin was invaded by giant rats.
(With revulsion)
That first night we lay awake and listened to them
scurrying and scratching behind the walls.

*THE LAME CHILD EDGES FURTHER FOWARD*

They were fearless!
They bit tiny babies, fought dogs: and killed cats...
...rats ate all our cheeses: and lapped-up soup,
ran over the furniture; and nested inside drawers.
And they gnawed gnawed everything in sight. Why!
There wasn't a hat or Sunday best bonnet
left without tell-tale holes.
(Smiling fleetingly)
The townsfolk were desperate.
They set traps, staked nets and laid trails of
poison... But.
(Shaking head)
All proved to be of little use.
(Sighing)

*THE LAME CHILD MOVES OVER TO THE STOOL*

**LAME CHILD:** By this time people were in despair...
and...

*THE LAME CHILD SITS AWKWARDLY*

...An angry crowd marched to the Market Square
and **demanded** that the Mayor rid the
town of rats.
(Pause)
The red-faced Mayor stood on the steps
of our fine Town Hall. And spluttered excuses!

*THE LAME CHILD LOOKS UP TO THE SIDE AND SMILES FULLY*

(With amazement)
At that very moment a willowy stranger
appeared from nowhere...
dressed from head to toe in a long coat,
half yellow, half red.
He stood close to me.
his eyes were needle-sharp, skin weathered and his
flaxen hair hung long and loose.
And his **smile; his** smile was magical and mysterious.
(Lifting an end of the black scarf)
I noticed a pipe hanging from the long striped scarf that he wore.
(Pause)
This, was the strangest figure any of us had ever seen.

*THE LAME CHILD LAYS THE CRUTCH DOWN CAREFULLY
AND VIEWS IT CRITICALLY*

This pied piper claimed that he could charm **all**
creatures, that creep, fly or run:
(Stretching out a hand)
and asked 1000 guilders to rid our town of rats.

*THE LAME CHILD ATTEMPTS TO STAND WITHOUT THE CRUTCH*

The Mayor accepted hastily: promised 50,000. The crowd cheered,
hats were thrown in the air.

*THE LAME CHILD SINKS BACK DOWN*

The piper smiled a small smile and his eyes twinkled.
The townsfolk... waited.
He blew three long shrill notes.

*THE LAME CHILD LOOKS FROM SIDE TO SIDE, LISTENS OUT*

(Quietly)
Muttering, scampering... from every cellar and attic.

| **LAME CHILD:** | (Louder, expressively)<br>Grumblings...<br>(Loud and extended)<br>**Rum**blings!<br>And with that, an army of squealing rats tumbled out of the houses. |
|---|---|

*THE LAME CHILD IS PICTURING THE SCENE, FINALLY SMILES*

The pied piper played until the last rat was out.
The beady-eyed monsters had fallen under the spell
of the piper's tune. And they streamed after him.
The Mayor stood rooted to the spot
as the pied piper led the mad procession through the streets.
(Pause)
The rats followed wherever **he** led.
They followed... to the river: plunged headlong into the swirling waters and were washed away.

*THE LAME CHILD TOYS WITH THE LONG SCARF*

Except for one... that somehow swam the wide river, and lived.

*THE LAME CHILD PICKS UP THE CRUTCH AND WAVES IT HIGH*

The church bells rang out; there was dancing in
the square. Mothers kissed sons and daughters
and fathers embraced wives; townsfolk were happy again!

*THE LAME CHILD SHRINKS BACK CRADLING THE CRUTCH*

I think the Mayor had all but forgotten the pied piper,
for he was looking very pleased with himself and boasting
of how **his** plan had ridded the town of vermin.
(Pause)
But the pied piper appeared and asked for the 1,000 guilders.
The Mayor laughed in his face, offered 50 for the silly tune.
'The very idea of paying a wanderer with a gypsy coat:
you must be mad!'

*THE LAME CHILD EXTENDS A HAND*

(Gently)
'You promised', replied the pied pipier and his face was sad.
(Shouting)
'Do you threaten us, fellow? Do your worst:
the rats are dead. What's dead can't come back to life!'
And with that the Mayor turned his back on the piper.
The pied piper smiled darkly.
(Quietly)
'Then I'll play a different tune.'

*THE LAME CHILD STANDS SUPPORTED BY THE CRUTCH*

**LAME CHILD:** He blew the softest notes imaginable.
The townsfolk looked uneasy.
(Pause)
Pattering, ...clattering wooden shoes.
And little hands clapping.
Those few notes promised more than I can ever tell.
We were bewitched by the enchanted pipe!

*THE LAME CHILD EDGES PITIFULLY TOWARDS THE SOUND*

Children were skipping from all over town.
We needed to be close to him.
(Proudly)
I danced past the Mayor, he had been struck dumb.
Mothers and Fathers found themselves unable to move,
unable to cry out.
The town emptied and we **laughed** as he led us
away through the forest.

*THE LAME CHILD TURNS TO CATCH A SOUND*

I thought I heard a distant voice calling us back;
but it drowned in our laughter.

*THE LAME CHILD MOVES A SHORT DISTANCE*

We laughed louder as the pied piper turned towards
the setting sun, the sky was streaked half red, half yellow.
(Pause)
I was slow; I heard the Mayor shouting,
'He'll be forced to stop; he'll never cross the mountains!'
(Scornfully)
They knew nothing of the pied piper's magic!
There was no way of stopping us as we danced to the piper's tune.
'We'll soon have our children back,' cried a mother.

*THE LAME CHILD SHAKES HEAD SADLY*

The pied piper played on.
Dusk was falling as the head of the procession
reached the mountain face.
Then, the strangest thing of all...
...The side of the mountain opened up!
(Bitterly)
I had fallen a long way behind.
Slower, younger children had been helped by the
older ones... even the youngest who could
barely walk had found willing hands.

**LAME CHILD:**   (Pause)
But I was too far back.
(Shouting)
'Wait for me!'
(Pause)
No one heard.
(Pause)
I had almost caught up: I saw the last few friends
disappear inside the cavern.
Then the music stopped.

*THE LAME CHILD BANGS THE CRUTCH HARD AGAINST THE FLOOR*

The mountain closed up as mysteriously as it had opened.
And I found myself alone.
(Pause)
I had been unable to dance the whole of the way.
I shall never see the wonderful place;
the place where everything is strange and new where I
would no longer be lame.

*THE LAME CHILD RETURNS TO THE STOOL AND SITS*

# MISSING PRESUMED DEAD

**NEWT IS A BRIGHT BUOYANT CHARACTER WITH EXTREMELY MOBILE FACE AND EXPRESSIVE GESTURES REMINISCENT OF A MAGICIAN. NEWT IS DRESSED CASUALLY IN BLACK.**

*AN EMPTY GOLDFISH BOWL FILLED WITH WATER (WITH AN ENORMOUS PACKET OF FISHFOOD STANDING BESIDE IT) DOMINATES A SMALL TABLE FRONT STAGE.*
*ENTER: NEWT, WALKING BACKWARDS IN ORDER TO REMAIN FACING AN UNSEEN OLDER SISTER (SIS IS SEATED OFF STAGE IN THE WINGS).*

**NEWT:**    (Sighing loudly)
All right! All right!
Keep your hair on, Sis.
So I forgot.
I'll feed it now.
(Louder exaggerated sigh)
I'm **not** neglecting my fish;
I fed Walter last night
before I went to bed.

*NEWT LISTENS ATTENTIVELY TO UNHEARD COMMENT*

(Quickly)
And what gives **you** the right
to boss me about all the time
just because you're older, anyway?

*PAUSE FOR A FURTHER SCATHING UNHEARD COMMENT*

(Muttering through clenched teeth)
Big deal.

*PAUSE FOR AN UNHEARD RETORT*

I'm on my way......

NEWT SAUNTERS OVER TO THE TABLE AND SPRINKLES FISHFOOD LIBERALLY WITH HARDLY A GLANCE AT THE GOLDFISH BOWL BEFORE TURNING AWAY: NEWT HESITATES – THEN FREEZES AND TURNS AROUND PAINFULLY SLOWLY STARING OPEN MOUTHED AT THE GOLDFISH BOWL

(With quavering voice)
Ssiss!
(A sharp intake of breath)
**Sis!**

*NEWT TURNS TO ADDRESS SIS DIRECTLY*

SIS!

*NEWT IS PERPLEXED AND LOOKS BACK TOWARDS THE TABLE*
*NEWT CONCENTRATES HARD ON THE GOLDFISH BOWL AND*
*PEERS THROUGH THE CURVED GLASS CLOSELY WITH GREAT*
*SUSPICION BEFORE MOVING ROUND AND PEERING INSIDE FROM*
*DIRECTLY ABOVE*

**NEWT:**
(Quietly)
It's not there.

*NEWT'S WORST FEARS HAVE BEEN CONFIRMED*

(Shouting)
Sis!  It's not there.

*NEWT STEPS BACKWARDS LOOKING MYSTIFIED*

It's GONE!

*NEWT SLIDES A HAND INTO THE WATER AND VIEWS WRIGGLING*
*MAGNIFIED FINGERS FROM THE OUTSIDE*
*NEWT STEPS BACK SHAKING HEAD AND WET HAND*

(Shouting)
My fish is missing.

*PAUSE FOR UNHEARD RETORT*

My fish has gone missing
I tell you.
(Defensively)
I'm NOT telling porky pies!
I'm NOT making it up!

*NEWT RUSHES OVER TO CONFRONT SIS*

What do you mean,
it cant've gone far!

*PAUSE FOR AN UNHEARD EXPLANATION*

(Shrugging shoulders)
I'll look...
(Pulling a face on turning)
...but I don't think so!

*NEWT RETURNS TO THE TABLE AND PRESCRIBES A WIDE ARC*
*FROM THE CENTRE OF THE GOLDFISH BOWL BEFORE PROCEEDING*
*TO SEARCH THE SURROUNDING FLOOR AREA*

(Addressing Sis loudly over one shoulder)
No!
Walter hasn't jumped out.
(Defeated)

**NEWT:** Yes! It would be equally true to say
that Walter is no longer inside.

*NEWT SCOWLS IN RESPONSE TO UNHEARD JIBE AND RACES OVER TO CONFRONT SIS*

(Adopting a hands-on-hip stance)
I don't need to be reminded
that I am in the habit of loosing things!
But I have NOT lost Walter.
(Dramatically)
The goldfish has ... vanished;
...not the same thing at all.

*NEWT STIFFENS AND STANDS VERY TALL*

**Don't** be ridiculous,
we haven't got a cat, have we?
(Pause)
It's no laughing matter.
Act your age, please!

*NEWT SHAKES HEAD IN NEGATIVE RESPONSE TO AN UNHEARD SUGGESTION*

(Sarcastically)
Yes!
Yes, makes for a brill trick, doesn't it!
(Pause)
If I only knew how to magic Walter back.

*NEWT MOVES PENSIVELY TOWARDS THE TABLE*

Perhaps I'll never know
what happened to Walter.
(Sighing loudly)
He might've been an average-lookIng
sort of goldfish
but he always had time for me;
he always had time to listen.

*NEWT SPINS AROUND*

What are you laughing at, Sis?
(Pause)
You're at the bottom of this, aren't you?
You've set me up!
You're laughing at me,
I know you are.
You know something that you're
not telling me about.

*NEWT POINTS AN ACCUSING FINGER*

**NEWT:**     (Shouting)
You've taken my fish, haven't you?
(Pause)
**ADMIT** IT!
You've hidden Walter somewhere!
Where?
Tell me!  Where?

*NEWT IS SUFFICIENTLY CALM TO LISTEN TO THE UNHEARD
EXPLANATION*

Yes......
...Yes, I knew Mum wanted Walter
to have a bigger home...
......Well?

*NEWT RACES PAST THE TABLE GRABBING THE FISHFOOD*

(Joyfully)
Mum, Sis says you've a surprise for me!

**EXIT NEWT**

## SOLO SCENES SERIES

**THE SIEVE and other scenes**

The first book of solo
scenes including an
adaptation of
THE LITTLE MATCH GIRL
ISBN 0 9522224 0 X

**CABBAGE and other scenes**

The second book of solo
scenes including an
adaptation of
THE PIED PIPER OF HAMELIN
ISBN 0 9522224 5 0

Dramatic Lines publications may be obtained
direct from the publishers or from booksellers.

---

To: **Dramatic Lines, PO Box 201, Twickenham TW2 5RQ, England**

Please send me......... ☐    copy/copies of **THE SIEVE** @ £4.99 each plus 80p p&p.

☐    copy/copies of **CABBAGE** @ £4.99 each plus 80p p&p.

*Please make cheque/PO payable to Dramatic Lines*

Name .......................................................................................................

Address ....................................................................................................

.......................................................................................................

.............................................. Postcode ....................................

Scenes fom **Cabbage** and **The Sieve** have won drama competitions and awards. The Publisher would be interested to hear of any success achieved using this material.

*Please send details to:*

Dramatic Lines
PO Box 201
Twickenham
TW2 5RQ
England

**Pears,** the first book of duologues by Heather Stephens will be available soon.